MXJC
12-11

HOW TELESCOPES, BINOCULARS, AND MICROSCOPES WORK

BY RYAN JACOBSON • ILLUSTRATED BY GLEN MULLALY

Published by The Child's World®
1980 Lookout Drive • Mankato, MN 56003-1705
800-599-READ • www.childsworld.com

ACKNOWLEDGMENTS
The Child's World®: Mary Berendes, Publishing Director
Content Consultant: Adam Green, PhD, Associate Professor
    of Physics, University of St. Thomas
The Design Lab: Design and production
Red Line Editorial: Editorial direction

LIBRARY OF CONGRESS
CATALOGING-IN-PUBLICATION DATA
Jacobson, Ryan.
  How telescopes, binoculars, and microscopes work /
by Ryan Jacobson ; illustrated by Glen Mullaly.
      p. cm.
  Includes bibliographical references and index.
  ISBN 978-1-60973-214-1 (library reinforced : alk. paper)
 1. Optical instruments—Juvenile literature. I. Mullaly,
Glen, 1968- ill. II. Title.
  QC371.4.J33 2012
  681'.4--dc22   2011010913

Photo Credits © iStockphoto, cover, 1, 21, 22, 23 (bottom),
24 (left), 24 (right), 25, 31; Fotolia, 8, 20, 26; Aaron Kohr/
Fotolia, 10; Alistair Cotton/Fotolia, 23 (top)

Printed in the United States of America in Mankato,
Minnesota.
July 2011
PA02092

ABOUT THE AUTHOR
Ryan Jacobson is a successful author
and presenter. He has written nearly 20
children's books—including picture books,
graphic novels, chapter books and choose-
your-path books—with several more
projects in the works. He has presented
at dozens of schools, organizations,
and special events. Ryan lives in Mora,
Minnesota, with his wife Lora, sons Jonah
and Lucas, and dog Boo. For more about
the author, please visit his website at
www.RyanJacobsonOnline.com.

ABOUT THE ILLUSTRATOR
Glen Mullaly draws neato pictures for kids
of all ages from his swanky studio on the
west coast of Canada. He lives with his
awesomely understanding wife and their
spectacularly indifferent cat. Glen loves
old books, magazines, and cartoons, and
someday wants to illustrate a book on How
Monsters Work!

TABLE OF CONTENTS

CHAPTER ONE

IT'S A BIRD . . . IT'S A PLANE . . .

Your cape flaps against your back. Your hair whips against your face. Clouds become a white blur as you soar through the sky. From miles below, you hear a desperate voice. "Help! Someone, please help!"

You focus your super vision on the source of the cry. It's your classmate, Gus Maroon. He's being chased by a pack of evil mutant science teachers! Is it a problem? Not for you. After all, you're Super Student!

This sounds like a story from a comic book. Of course, there are no evil mutant science teachers. (We think.) And, you can't fly or hear shouts from

miles away. But, with the help of special tools, you *can* see things that are very small or far away. Thanks to telescopes, binoculars, and microscopes, you can see the world like a superhero.

Today, you may use these tools in school, or even for fun. If you lived a few years ago, or even 1,000 years ago, would you be using them?

20 YEARS AGO

The Hubble Space Telescope was put into orbit around Earth. This telescope gathers images from space that have never been seen before. It takes pictures of distant galaxies that cannot be seen from telescopes on Earth.

150 YEARS AGO

By now, binoculars had been around for a few years. They were becoming more popular and were used by soldiers during the US Civil War.

300 YEARS AGO

People had been able to **magnify** objects for many years. But now, microscopes were important tools in science. Scientists used them to learn more about the tiny things around them.

400 YEARS AGO

Galileo Galilei became the first person to study the night sky using a telescope. With it, he discovered that the moon's surface is bumpy. He also found out that Jupiter has moons.

1,000 YEARS AGO

The reading stone was invented. It was the world's first known vision aid. Like a magnifying glass, the reading stone was a piece of curved glass. It made written words look bigger and easier to read.

BACK TO TODAY

Telescopes, binoculars, and microscopes are used all around the world. Telescopes help us peer into the night sky. Binoculars allow a closer look for bird watching and other outdoor hobbies. Microscopes help scientists develop cures for diseases and help police solve crimes.

CHAPTER TWO

LET THERE BE LIGHT!

Telescopes, binoculars, and microscopes are amazing tools. But how do they work? To find out, you first need to know more about light.

Look around. The lights are on, and you can see all around. How? Invisible light rays are passing through the air. They travel from a source, such as a lamp or the sun. When light rays hit something, like your best

friend's face, they bounce off it. When this light reaches your eyes, you're able to see her funny smile.

Light travels faster than anything else in the universe. A ray of light can circle Earth more than seven times in one second! Still, it can be blocked by some things—like a brick wall or your brother's head. It can be bent by other stuff, such as glass or plastic.

Lens Bends

In a telescope, binoculars, or a microscope, a glass piece called a **lens** bends light. By bending light, a lens can change an image in a number of ways. Often, a lens magnifies an image, or it turns it upside down.

Tourist binoculars offer an up-close view of a city skyline.

CONCAVE OR CONVEX?

There are two types of lenses. They bend light differently and are used in different ways.

A *concave* lens curves inward. When light rays pass through this lens, they move away from each other. A movie projector has a concave lens. The light moves through the lens and spreads out to fill the screen.

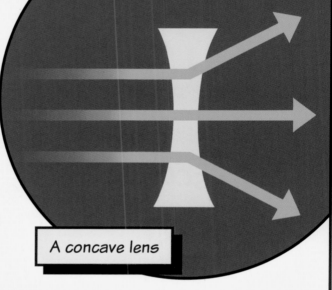

A concave lens

A *convex* lens curves outward. Light rays that pass through this lens come together. They meet at a point on the opposite side of the lens. A convex lens can make things look bigger.

A convex lens

BIGGIES

Larger telescopes gather more light than smaller ones. These telescope giants can see a lot more stars and galaxies in the night sky. The objective lens of the Gran Telescopio Canarias is 34 feet (10 m) wide! Four million eyeballs would be needed to collect as much light as this telescope does. That's because your eyes collect light through tiny holes called pupils. You can think of a telescope as a big eyeball with a big pupil.

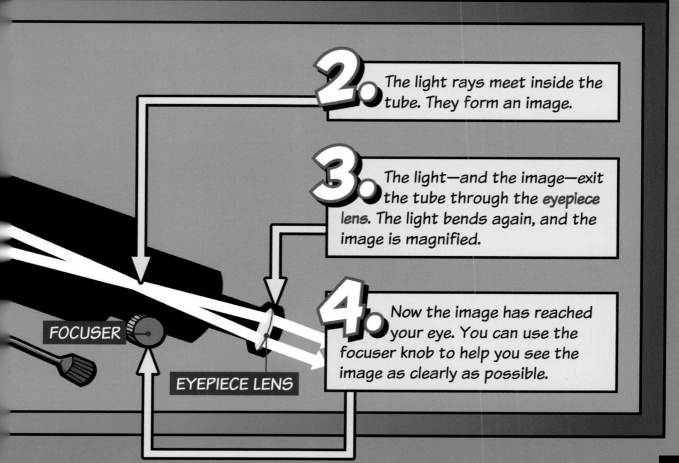

2. The light rays meet inside the tube. They form an image.

3. The light—and the image—exit the tube through the eyepiece lens. The light bends again, and the image is magnified.

4. Now the image has reached your eye. You can use the focuser knob to help you see the image as clearly as possible.

FOCUSER

EYEPIECE LENS

BINOCULARS

Binoculars are basically two telescopes put together. But, there are some different parts.

4. The eyepiece lenses catch the image and magnify it for you to see. This happens on each side of the binoculars.

EYEPIECE LENSES

PRISMS

THUMBSCREW

2. The image is bounced off a glass **prism** and flips onto its side.

OBJECTIVE LENS

1. Light passes through the objective lens. The light rays bend so much that the object appears upside down.

3. This sideways image reflects off a second prism. The image flips again. Now it is right side up.

INDEPENDENT FOCUS

5. You can twist the independent focus. This adjusts the focus on each side of the binoculars.

You can turn the thumbscrew to adjust the distance between the eyepiece and the objective lens. This brings the image into focus.

WHAT DO THOSE NUMBERS MEAN?

Binoculars can be described using two numbers, such as 7 x 42. The first number tells you the magnification. In this case, the binoculars magnify an object to look seven times (7x) larger. The second number tells you the size of the objective lens—42 millimeters in this example. The bigger the lens, the better the binoculars work in dark places, such as forests.

MICROSCOPES

Microscopes are a bit different from telescopes and binoculars. They point downward instead of up and out. And, they use mirrors. A compound microscope, like the one below, has two or more lenses.

EYEPIECE LENS

FINE-ADJUSTMENT KNOB

BODY TUBE

COURSE-ADJUSTMENT KNOB

ARM

OBJECTIVE LENS

STAGE

1. A mirror near the bottom of the microscope reflects light up.

BASE

5. Light passes through the eyepiece lens. The object is magnified a second time before the light enters your eye.

The fine-adjustment knob helps bring samples into focus. The course-adjustment knob lets you move the body tube to better see different samples.

4. The objective lens magnifies the object's image inside the body tube.

3. Light passes through the object on its way to the objective lens.

2. The light shines through a hole in the stage, or shelf. This is where the object is placed.

GREAT PIX!

Scientists can take pictures of what they see through a microscope. They use digital cameras, which may be similar to one your family owns. These cameras allow scientists to save their pictures on a computer. Then, the scientists can look at the images more carefully.

HOW MUCH BIGGER?

Just how much bigger do microscopes make things look? The answer depends on the lenses. Let's say you're looking at a rare bug in a microscope. The objective lens magnifies the bug ten times (10x). That means the bug will look ten times bigger by the time it gets to the eyepiece lens. Now, let's say the eyepiece lens magnifies four times (4x). It will make the 10x image even bigger—four times bigger to be exact. To figure out the total magnification, you have to do a math problem. Multiply the lenses' magnifications together: 10 x 4 = 40. In this case, the answer would be 40x.

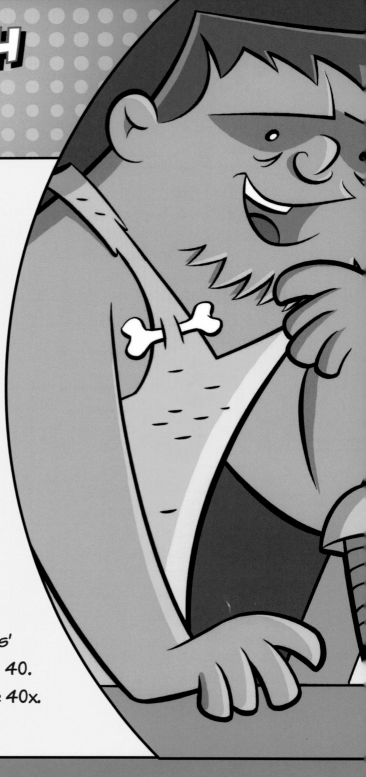

Microscope, Please!

You're the most brilliant scientist alive. And, you're about to make a discovery that will change the world forever. "Get me a microscope," you tell your assistant. "And hurry!"

The assistant replies, "What kind?"

Microscopes come in many kinds. Scientists choose the type of microscope depending on what they're studying. Here are some of their choices:

- Compound microscope: This is the most common type of microscope. It has two or more lenses. It's good for looking at things such as insects, seeds, and fingerprints.
- Dark-field microscope: Light reflects off

A researcher adjusts a compound microscope for a better look.

an object, so it appears bright against a dark background. This is a great microscope for studying bacteria.

- Phase-contrast microscope: Light bends differently through different parts of an object. Scientists can more clearly see the parts that make up a cell or a tiny living thing.

A fluorescent microscope uses light in many ways.

- Fluorescent microscope: Objects glow with different colors of light. Scientists can see tiny creatures in 3-D.

Other, more complicated types of microscopes allow scientists to see objects as small as atoms.

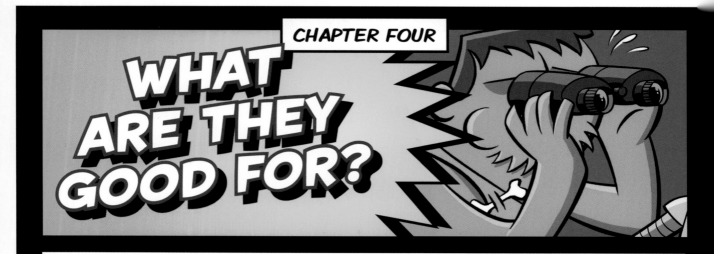

CHAPTER FOUR

WHAT ARE THEY GOOD FOR?

Now you know how they work, but what are these tools used for?

Telescopes

What can you really see with a decent, home telescope? Well, don't expect to see amazingly clear and bright images like the ones in your favorite astronomy magazine. Even so, a basic telescope lets you see some pretty cool stuff.

TIME LINE

ABOUT 5000 BC
People traveling through Africa discover how to make glass.

ABOUT 3500 BC
People in Egypt begin making beads and vases out of glass.

ABOUT 100 AD
Roman inventors experiment with glass. They discover how lenses work.

ABOUT 1000
The reading stone is invented to magnify written words.

1. The moon's surface: You'll be able to see the moon's craters and mountains in good detail.
2. The planets: You can see four of Jupiter's biggest moons, and Saturn's rings will dazzle you. Neptune will look like a small blue dot. Still, your telescope is the only way to see that distant planet.
3. The stars, kind of: They'll look brighter, maybe, but not that much larger.
4. NOT the sun: Don't look at the sun unless your telescope has a special filter.

ABOUT 1284
Italian inventor Salvino D'Armate creates the world's first eyeglasses.

1595
Two Dutch eyeglass makers use lenses and a tube to build an invention similar to a telescope.

1608
Holland's Jan Lippershey invents binoculars.

1609
Galileo Galilei creates his own telescope.

Binoculars

Sure, it's fun to spy on your friend down the street. But why else do people have binoculars?

1. Bird watching: A pair of binoculars offers a close-up view of birds without scaring them away. Bird watching is the fastest growing outdoor activity in the United States.
2. Hunting: A good pair of binoculars can help a hunter spot a distant target. Some can even tell hunters exactly how far away the animal is.
3. Sightseeing: Many travelers love binoculars. There's nothing like zooming in on the bottom of the Grand Canyon or a distant waterfall.
4. Sporting events: Live sporting events are a blast, but the view from stadium seats can be a bummer. Binoculars are the perfect addition for the big game.

1674
Anton van Leeuwenhoek develops lenses that magnify better than ever before. He will become known as the "Father of Microscopy."

1668
Sir Isaac Newton invents the reflector telescope. This allows objects to be magnified millions of times.

1830
Joseph Jackson Lister creates the first compound microscope.

1931
The electron microscope is invented. This allows scientists to see objects as small as an atom.

1981
Gerd Binnig and Heinrich Rohrer invent the scanning tunneling microscope, the strongest microscope yet.

1990
The Hubble Space Telescope begins orbiting Earth.

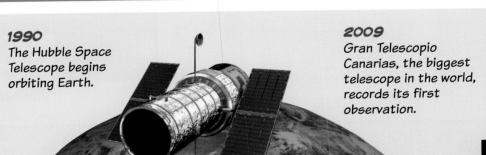

2009
Gran Telescopio Canarias, the biggest telescope in the world, records its first observation.

Microscopes

What about microscopes? You can examine bugs with them. But what else are they for?

1. The study of life: Scientists use microscopes to look at anything from pine needles to spider parts. They also study bacteria and viruses—those germs that make living things sick.

2. Catching criminals: Forensic scientists study tiny pieces of evidence from a crime scene—fingerprints, clothing, hair, and more. Microscopes can even tell if the same gun fired two different bullets.

3. Helping Earth: Scientists use microscopes to examine polluted water or soil.

4. Finding cures: Doctors and medical researchers are always looking for new and better ways to cure diseases. They use microscopes to see how different medicines affect germs.

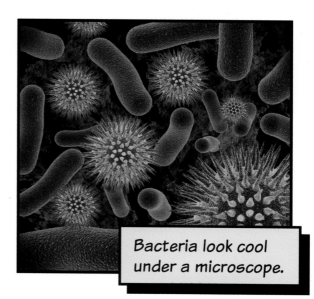

Bacteria look cool under a microscope.

CHAPTER FIVE

I WANT THAT!

All right, so you're convinced—telescopes, binoculars, and microscopes are awesome! And now you want one of each, right? There's just a tiny problem: You need to decide what kind to get. Keep these tips in mind as you shop:

Choosing a Telescope

- A decent, basic telescope can be quite expensive— good binoculars cost a lot less. Before you shell out for a telescope, ask yourself what you're hoping to see. A pair of binoculars is great for looking at constellations in your backyard.

- If you're still sure you want a telescope, make sure it fits in the space you have. They can get quite large, so measure ahead of time.
- Don't forget a good, sturdy mount. Asking your little brother to hold it for you just won't cut it. Your telescope has to be quite still for you to use it well.
- Beware of "high-powered" telescopes. The telescope may be powerful, but the image will be blurry and faint.
- There are a lot of good, used telescopes out there. Consider buying used and saving more than half the price of a new one.

ALL THE DETAILS, PLEASE

It might seem like telescopes, binoculars, and microscopes are all about making small things look bigger. But there's something else that's just as important—a clear picture. Scientists often need to examine objects that are really close together. They don't want to see one big blob—they need to see each object on its own.

Choosing Binoculars

- Make sure your binoculars feel good to hold. You don't want them to be too big or too heavy.
- More magnification isn't always better. If your binoculars are too powerful, it will be hard to keep them focused. You probably want a magnification of 10x or less. An 8 x 42 pair of binoculars is likely your best bet.

- Know when and where you'll most often use your binoculars. Are you planning to use them in dark, shaded areas or at sunrise and sunset? If so, you'll want binoculars with a large objective lens. If your plan is to look at birds in your sunny backyard, a smaller lens will work better.

Choosing a Microscope

Here you have two main choices—compound microscope or dissecting microscope. You already know how a compound microscope works. It magnifies better than a dissecting microscope.

In a dissecting microscope, light doesn't come up from below the object. Instead, light shines from above. That means you can study thicker objects, and you can see colors better.

Which kind is best for you? To find out, decide what you'll look at the most. Is it stuff like coins and rocks? If so, you'll probably prefer a dissecting microscope. Or are you more interested in things like tiny seeds and insects? In that case, a compound microscope is for you.

A SCIENTIST'S WISH LIST

So, you want to be a scientist. Here is a list of supplies you might need for your microscope:

- Microscope slides—to put your specimen on while you study it.
- Tweezers—to grab and move tiny specimens.
- Eyedropper—to add water or dye to your specimen, if needed.
- Lens paper—to clean your microscope lenses and slides.
- Notebook, pen, and pencil—to record your findings.
- Clear plastic ruler—to measure your specimen.
- Scissors—to cut your specimen.

WORDS TO KNOW

concave (kon-KAYV): If something is concave, it curves inward. A concave lens causes light rays to spread out as they pass through.

convex (KON-veks): If something is convex, it curves outward. A convex lens causes light rays to bend inward as they pass through.

eyepiece lens (EYE-peess LENZ): An eyepiece lens is the lens in telescopes, binoculars, and microscopes that a user looks through. An eyepiece lens helps magnify an object.

lens (LENZ): A lens is a piece of curved glass or plastic that bends light rays. Telescopes, binoculars, and microscopes have more than one lens.

magnify (MAG-nuh-FYE): To magnify means to make something appear larger. Telescopes, binoculars, and microscopes magnify objects.

objective lens (ub-JEC-tiv LENZ): An objective lens is the lens in telescopes, binoculars, and microscopes closest to the object being studied. The objective lens bends light bouncing off an object.

prism (PRIZ-um): A prism is an object that can bend light and flip an image. A prism in binoculars is a wedge of glass.

INDEX

FIND OUT MORE

Visit our Web site for links about how telescopes, binoculars, and microscopes work: childsworld.com/links

Note to Parents, Teachers, and Librarians: We routinely verify our Web links to make sure they are safe and active sites. So encourage your readers to check them out!